Best College Match

Gregory and Opal Dawson

BK
ROYSTON
Publishing

BK Royston Publishing
502-802-5385 | www.bkroystonpublishing.com

Cover Design: Bill Lacy
Back Cover Photo Credit: Marvin Young

ISBN-13: 978-1-946111-05-0
ISBN-10: 1-946111-05-8

Printed in the United States of America

Table Of Contents

Mission Statement

Our mission is to provide students the understanding to obtain greater success in life through graduation from the right college at the right price by helping them realize their "Best College Match."

We do this through a proven 5 step 'Best M. A. T. C. H.' process where students learn to:

1. **M**aster knowledge of "personal" self-awareness

2. **A**ccept ownership of academic "proficiencies"

3. **T**houghtfully identify college "parameters"

4. **C**arefully "procure" college funding

5. **H**onestly "pick" the *'Best College Match'*

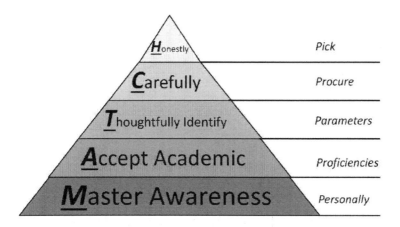

Introduction

Time is the greatest resource that any of us has so, let me get straight to the point.

This book is about one thing, increasing your "Life's Success" through identifying, funding and choosing your 'Best College Match.'

<u>The transition from high school to adulthood is undoubtedly one of the biggest milestones in life</u> and must be approached as such because the stakes are high and the path is often unclear.

More importantly, if we are to experience a successful life, we must decisively master exactly what we are going to achieve after high school. How we approach this huge life decision will largely determine the quality of the future lives we will lead.

Therefore, we believe that our post-high school education is inextricably tied to many of life's biggest decisions, including career aspirations, financial goals, marital status and plans for a family.

Also, we believe some other great benefits of a good college education besides access to significant financial opportunities are to accomplish two other very important life goals.

1) College teaches us how to think critically about the world.

2) College prepares us to effectively participate in the global economy.

As our son approached the end of his high school career, we began to understand the difficulty surrounding how to best balance the transition from high school to college. At first, it was an abstract idea, but when he became serious about furthering his education the overwhelming amount of choices that he had to decide upon became a huge challenge to overcome. He had to decide where and why he wanted to go to a specific school and how he was going to pay for it.

We've always been close and as he would mention possible schools, we would challenge him on the specific "whys" of how a particular college would be the 'Best College Match' for him. Through our initial discussions, subsequent research and work (of which this book is the result,) he soon moved beyond* the knee jerk thoughts of "because we like their team," "it's popular," "it has a great reputation," "many of my friends are going," and the proverbial "they're giving me money."

Later, he began to see that, yes, these were all reasons but not the best reasons to choose a particular college. As we dove deeper into which colleges would best suit him, we came up with a list of the 5 most important steps in determining your 'Best College Match'.

See Blake's Story of receiving over $1,000,000 in college scholarships at www.bestcollegematch.com

The 5 "Most Important" Steps For Determining Your Best College Match

(M.A.T.C.H. the 5 P's of transitioning from high school to college)

1. **P**ersonal Self Awareness

2. **P**roficiencies in Academics

3. **P**arameters of College Choices

4. **P**rocure of College Funding

5. **P**ick The 'Best College Match'

If you've been on top of your game and have done a good job of managing these steps then congratulations. Use the information in this book to grow and expand on the knowledge that you already possess.

If you feel that you are behind schedule or haven't begun to develop your college basis around these 5 steps, it's not too late. Get busy, and use this information to develop and grow your college basis to find your *"Best College Match."*

You Hold the Power

By understanding and implementing each of these 5 steps, you will increase your level of personal ownership. You will successfully navigate through steps and enhance the chances for a smooth transition from high school to college. In addition, increasing your level of personal ownership enhances your level of confidence. Thus, you have a greater chance for success in all aspects of life.

The outcomes of "Life Success" that you reap are all up to you.

Therefore, don't become too burdened with this very important task. When you understand the reasons for your choices then the decisions become easier and lead you to make impactful and positive changes in your life which will bring greater "Life Success."

The decision is not simply to just go to college – a college, any college – but to go to the 'Best College Match' for you based on your greatest understanding of what choosing the best college for you means.

We've written this book because when you've completed it, we want you to be able to say with complete **CONFIDENCE** that:

1.   I know myself well (I value myself **P**ersonally)

2.   I own my academic record (I understand my **P**roficiencies)

3.   I have identified colleges that fit (I have selected college within my **P**arameters)

4.   I have acceptable college funding (I'm paying for college with **P**rocured funding)

5.   I have chosen the college for me (I've **P**icked my 'Best College Match')

Here's The Point.

You may already have an action plan around transitioning from high school to college and that is great!

However, we believe that after reading this book, you will have a better understanding of yourself, and you will have a more focused, purposeful, and well-thought out plan that empowers you to make substantial changes in your life, both educationally and personally. This winning spirit can lead you to greater happiness and "Life Success."

It's a spirit worth fighting for.

BEST
COLLEGE
MATCH

Step 1

Master Knowledge of "Personal" Self-Awareness

Personal Assessment

In this opening step, you will learn how to see, understand, and become more aware of your true personal character because as you transition from high school to college the strength of your *Personal Profile* will form the basis of your life for many years to come.

The type of person you are is important because even with all the excitement of looking forward to graduation, the fact is that the training wheels are coming off soon. And so, like never before in your life, *character really matters*.

Too often these days, college planning has become passé. The gravity of the responsibility involved in your decisions affects your ability to choose wisely. So, understanding all the necessary components toward achieving your "Best College Match" needs serious consideration. When you have a better sense of who you are and how your personal character influences your choices then you will make better decisions and increase the quality of your future.

A Tale of Two Students

Tommy is a celebrated student with top grades, very high test scores, and an outstanding resume of awards, accomplishments, and experiences.

Tammy is an accomplished student in her own right. She takes many of the same classes with Tommy who usually does somewhat better than her. Although Tammy does have decent grades and test scores along with a focused resume, she, as good a student, would in most cases, however, not be considered the high quality student scholar that Tommy is.

But . . . at the close of their senior year of high school, Tammy actually has more funding opportunities and scholarships because of her 'Best College Match' choices than does her higher caliber student classmate.

Tommy, on the other hand, has actually been accepted to some of the most prestigious universities in the land. Imagine that.

Although he is very excited and proud to have been accepted to these great colleges, he is extremely concerned that he's not going to be able to pay for the cost at any of these great schools because he hasn't received ample

2

college funding at these very expensive schools. Tommy is considering student loans, but he finds the idea of having to repay the debt extremely daunting.

How can this happen? Being smart and getting into a top university is supposed to be a good thing, right? Well, yes, it is. However, the cost of college has simply sky-rocketed and continues to increase every day, which makes most colleges out of financial range for many students without some additional funding support.

Tammy is awarded scholarships and other financial aid even though she received lesser grades than Tommy throughout her high school career.

So what's going on here? *Why is the "great" student doing poorly and the "decent" student doing very well in getting scholarships for college?*

Well, to answer the question, our top scholar Tommy is caught smack dab in the middle of the classic college educational dilemma. Tommy, as a hard working "scholar," works diligently to increase his academic record (head.)

While our friend, Tammy, is in quite another position. Tammy is strong scholastically in her own right, but she, as a more "self-aware" student, exercises high personal initiative (heart) too.

The reality is that both our students are actually very smart in their own ways.

However, Tommy is not realizing the adequate levels of college funding he might otherwise expect for a student of his caliber because he is selling his great academic record in the wrong, very narrow and highly competitive college and scholarship market. He doesn't understand the value of personal engagement in winning scholarships for college as is determined in the educational marketplace.

While at the same time, though she might be considered the lesser student to some degree, Tammy not only understands how admissions and funding packages are awarded, but she took the personal initiative to best position herself in a "win-win" situation based upon that knowledge.

Tammy worked hard to position herself accordingly, and she's done well because she is realizing what avenues to take to procure the proper or sufficient funding needed to support her "*Best College Match*."

The bigger fact of the matter is as smart as they are at their own things alone - the academically advanced Tommy and the motivated and self-aware Tammy both could greatly benefit from expanding their existing skill sets. Tammy could work harder in school, and Tommy could spend more time personally engaged with his college planning.

Thus, we see two students with two different outcomes based on their limited understandings of how to approach finding their 'Best College Match'.

Know this: in the real world, you can run but you can't hide behind a great reputation.

The point here is to . . .

"Be more concerned with your character than your reputation, because your character is what you really are, while your reputation is merely what others think you are." -John Wooden

Until this point in your educational careers, your strong academic record, special talent, or social reputation may have served you well in receiving a "reputational-pass." We hope you enjoyed it because those days are quickly coming to an end, and you will no longer receive any extra favor based on your reputation alone.

Personal Self Awareness – The New You

When you complete applications for colleges and scholarships, the training wheels are coming off, and everyone participating in the process must be at their true academic and personal best to stand out among the other strong applicants.

Therefore, as you transition into college, it will serve you well to be completely honest with yourself about your own character. We know this notion can be somewhat scary and even a little hard but if you want the best for yourself then you're going to have to do it.

The easiest way to do this is give yourself the room to listen to your inner-voice, which includes the intellectual you (head) and the emotional, social, and spiritual you (heart,) so that you can become the best "New You."

The more proficient you become at balancing the "New You" of your head (academic abilities) and your heart (personal character) through the continued development of your "*Personal Profile*," the better you will fare through the college application process.

The reality is that most serious college applicants are somewhere roughly between Tommy and Tammy, given their own *"Personal Profile."* Why? Because most ardent scholars aren't blowing off ways to best fund college and most well-adjusted, super self-aware students aren't blowing off everything else to find ways to fund college.

As we've seen, even the brightest students like Tommy can come up "short" if they aren't appropriately and personally engaged in the college application process.

Knowing who you are as a whole person matters because it will take getting the best out of the "New You" to most successfully find your "Best College Match."

Therefore, when it comes to being your best new You, character supersedes competency.

Let's begin with the personal profile.

Personal Profile

Commitment

	Lower	Higher
Higher	Place Holders	Rock Stars
Lower	Slackers	Up & Comers

Responsibility

The 4 Personal Character Types

Rock Stars are Highly Committed & Highly Responsible students who are "in it to win it." They are motivated, proactive, self-directed individuals who are engaged and involved in their personal self-development.

Place Holders are Less Committed & Highly Responsible students who are "going through the motions." They are poorly motivated, reactive, self-directed individuals who are less engaged, but still involved in their personal self-development.

Up & Comers are Highly Committed & Less Responsible students who are "works in progress." They are highly motivated, proactive, self-directed individuals who are highly engaged and poorly involved in their personal self-development.

Slackers are <u>Less Committed & Less Responsible</u> students who are "entitled and self-centered." They are poorly motivated, reactive, self-directed individuals who are poorly engaged and poorly involved in their personal self-development.

Once you understand which personality type you exhibit in your life then you can alter the aspects of yourself that aren't effectively leading you towards a successful future. Beyond simply understanding your *"Personal Profile,"* your ability to use it effectively requires that you be honest with yourself. Your personal character forms the foundation for your *"Best College Match."*

For this reason, we totally agree that . . .

"A winner is someone who recognizes his God-given talents, works his tail off to develop them into skills, and uses these skills to accomplish his goals." - Larry Bird

So, be prepared, as the "<u>New You</u>," to work your tail off as we move forward to find your "Best College Match."

Step 2

Accept Ownership of Academic "Proficiencies"

Personal Competencies

In this step, you will learn to understand, own, and align your academic record because colleges will judge you based upon your academic proficiencies. When your academic record is strong relative to others, you can increase your future educational opportunities.

Who's On First?

As we've learned, personal character – your *"Personal Profile"* – always matters because it is the basis of our lives.

However, more and more jobs require potential employees to possess higher levels of education; therefore, your academic record impacts the entire "Best College Match" process.

Your Academic Profile is most <u>relevant </u>in finding your "Best College Match" because it puts you on your way, but your *Personal Profile* is most <u>important</u> because it sustains you throughout your entire life's journey and not just your academic aspirations.

The overall quality of your personal *'Academic Profile'* (record) plus your *Personal Profile* will direct you to your most realistic and immediate future educational opportunities and thus your future Life Success.

Your *Academic Profile* quantifies your academic competency. Colleges utilize this profile as a primary indicator of potential college success; however, the secondary indicators colleges look at include a comprehensive approach, representing both the academic and the personal, so it is imperative that your *"Personal Profile"* exhibits the essential qualities needed to be successful on all levels, both in college and beyond.

Your Academic Record: You Only Get One So Make It Count!

Colleges and scholarship committees want to see strength represented in your educational background. To obtain this information, they will generally request your transcript and ACT / SAT scores. They will use this information to determine if your basic *"Academic Profile"* meets with their requirements.

Although there is varying criteria utilized to evaluate the viability of a college or scholarship application, the below four are the most widely used to assess an applicant's basic qualifications:

1.   Grades in college preparatory classes

2.   Grades in all classes

3.   Overall rigor of the curriculum

4.   College board exam scores (ACT/ SAT)

Your Academic Profile consists of (2) very important interrelated parts that define your academic record in relationship to:

1.   Competency – the rigor of your classes and your ACT / SAT test scores

2.   Performance – the grades you earned (your GPA) in the classes you took, which largely answers for colleges and scholarship committees their basic questions of, "How rigorously was this applicant challenged," and "How did he/she perform?"

The overall average Academic Profile threshold requirements of grades and test scores varies greatly between colleges and scholarship committees, but the methodology in judging the applicant's overall academic record as compared to what they are looking for in their student applicant pool remains the same.

Therefore, the students who are the most successful at realizing their 'Best College Match' are also the most proficient in understanding and aligning (and later selling) their personal *Academic Profile* (record) with the requirements needed to meet or exceed the college and scholarship expectations.

The fact is colleges and scholarship committees use your "*Academic Profile*" to make objective judgments about your academic proficiency (the type of student you are,) and subjective judgments about your personal character (the type of person you are) as outlined.

Academic Profile
Student Type

	Low	High
High	**Casuals** (Under Motivated)	**Scholars** (High Achieving)
Low	**Unprovens** (Unknown)	**Strivers** (Hardworking)

Performance

Students / Person Types

1.   Casuals – under-challenged, did well (Under Motivated)

2.   Scholars – highly-challenged, did well (High Achieving)

3.   Unprovens – under-challenged, not so well (Unknown)

4.   Strivers – highly-challenged, not so well (Hard Working)

Ultimately, what colleges and scholarship committees really want to know is if you are the caliber of student that would fit academically at their institution, as well as, if you are also the type of student that would enrich the overall value of their college community inside and outside of the classroom.

To that end, it should be obvious that all high school grades and classes aren't equal. An "A" in TV Appreciation is absolutely not the same thing as an "A" in Trigonometry,

Biology or Spanish II. So, being honest about the "New You" and how it relates to your academic competencies can make you or break you.

The fact is that your Junior Year "*Academic Profile*" is what colleges and scholarship committees will be judging because your Senior-year mid-term grades won't be available to utilize due to application deadlines in many instances.

Certainly, you can load up on Advanced Placement (AP) Classes and get all A's in them your Senior Year where mathematically it can increase your GPA overall, but not maybe as much as you might want depending on where you started.

Your other, and likely greater, option to improve your overall '*Academic Profile*' would be to retake your college boards. Because given the time, energy, and quite often money you can increase your ACT / SAT scores significantly.

Therefore, after you've done everything you can to build as strong an '*Academic Profile*' as possible, take ownership. No matter whether the '*Academic Profile*" is considered strong, weak or average, "own it" it's yours. Do your absolute best to make it work.

16

Making Your *"Academic Profile"* Work

Making your personal *"Academic Profile"* (record) work means that you understand that:

1. It's based on my grades and my college boards ACT/SAT scores

2. Once it's completed, my record is fixed and I "own it"

3. It defines the general parameters of my college and scholarship opportunities

4. It can be positively enhanced with additional supporting documentation

5. It's the major qualifier in comparing applicants for colleges and scholarships

6. It must be strategically aligned with the colleges you are applying to be most successful

Chart Your Personal *"Academic Profile"*

The chart *below* has been added to show you how to chart your own personal "Academic Profile" where all you need to do is make a dot on the chart where your GPA and your ACT / SAT scores intersect.

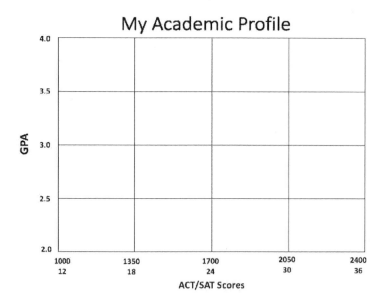

Understanding Your Academic Profile

Thus, like our friend Tammy, whatever your own personal *"Academic Profile"* turns out to be, you will need to best understand it and align it to the college that is the most realistic and advantageous for you so that you can present yourself successfully to prospective colleges and earn the needed scholarships.

Therefore, to get the "Best College Match," know your *Academic Profile* and seek to match it with the colleges that will benefit you the most.

Aligning Your Academic Profile

Thus, a smart rule of thumb is that – given your own GPA and Scores – your personal *"Academic Profile"* should be roughly greater than or equal to the average academic record among all applicants before you consider any additional supporting documentation. Said another way, your *'Academic Profile'* should be generally between ***the 50th to 100th percentile of the colleges or scholarships "Application Profile" for all applicants*** before any other considerations.

We generally disagree with the notion of applying to colleges and scholarships where the applicant's general *Academic Profile* is any lower than 50 percent because the student's probability of success will also be significantly lower. In addition, if or when an applicant is accepted, he/she may not be offered sufficient compensation packages

19

because the applicant does not compete at the level of other students on that campus. Additionally, as it relates to the highly competitive nature of winning scholarships, if the applicant is not at least as strong as 50% of those applying, what would be the real chances of that applicant winning the scholarship?

Of course, there are always exceptions based on any number of different circumstances, including an exceptional talent, skill, or ability, etc. that would make applying, and quite possibly winning, more probable.

However, the bottom line is this . . .

to be most successful in finding your "Best College Match" you need to be honest and realistic about your '*Academic Profile*' and stay in your academic lane!!!

Avoid Overreaching

The "Best College Match" process is successful because we teach students how to avoid applying to "Reach Schools," where they would be more unlikely to be accepted or gain significant funding packages. **We do this by encouraging**

our students to stay in their own academic lanes. By aligning their personal "Academic Profiles" to match a minimum of at least 50% of that of the average *"Academic Profile"* for all applicants, where the resulting "Relative Competitive Record" for their *"Best College Match"* applications are at least competitive enough to increase the chance for success.

We help our students strengthen their applications by 1) knowing who they are personally and 2) by knowing what their academic competencies are as students. Therefore, we are able to help you make wiser choices in finding your *"Best College Match"* fit because your *"Academic Profile"* will be better aligned to produce a more competitive "Relative Competitive Record" to realize greater admission rates and greater funding packages.

Thus, by aligning your *"Academic Profile"* in this manner, your "Relative Competitive Record" will immediately be at least as good as or better than average among all applicants within a given applicant pool.

Additionally, your *"Academic Profile"* can be aligned at higher or lower percentiles of the overall applicant pool to make your personal *"Relative Academic Record"* more or less competitive depending on your personal objectives.

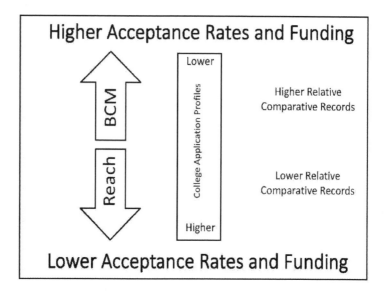

Align And Do Fine!

For example, Joe's GPA is 3.70 and he scored a 26 on his ACT. He compiled his *"Academic Profile"* without best aligning his *"Academic Profile"* before he applied to a top *"Ivy-Like"* college via the Application Profile as illustrated.

Joe's Misaligned Application Profile

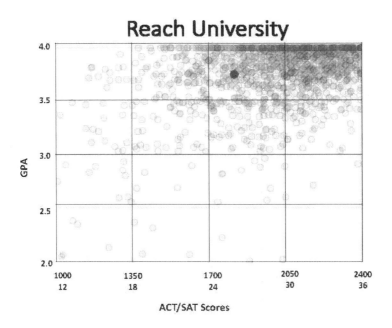

Unsurprisingly, Joe was not accepted because his "*Academic Profile*" was completely misaligned with the college's "Application Profile." Given his desperately low 'Relative Competitive Record' as compared to most other applicants, Joe, with no extraordinary special talents to justify admission into that school, was totally out of his academic lane in applying to this particular college.

However, Joe, after becoming a great student of the "Best College Match" process was able to gain acceptance and funding at a strong regional university with an "Application Profile" that was much more comparatively aligned with Joe's "Academic Profile" as shown.

Joe's Aligned Application Profile

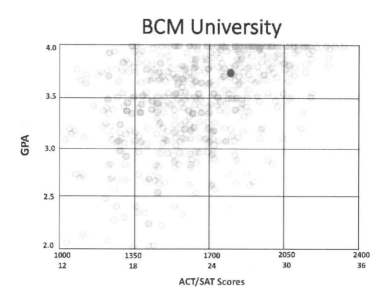

Happily, Joe was accepted this time because his "Academic Profile" was more strongly aligned with the college's *"Application Profile."* Joe's "Relative Comparative Record," as compared to other applicants, was much more competitive, which resulted in Joe's acceptance and funding in a more suitable *"Best College Match."* Given his much better *"Academic Profile"* alignment, Joe was totally in his academic lane in applying to this college.

Therefore, to vastly increase the chances of finding and funding your "Best College Match," students must do (3) specific things to best utilize their own personal *"Academic Profile:"*

1. **Own** – your *"Academic Profile"* because we only get one.

2. **Understand** – how your "Academic Profile" is used in determining future academic opportunities

3. **Align** – your "Academic Profile" strategically based on admissions requirements (stay in your lane)

Because when you best own, understand and align your "Academic Profile" you are best utilizing your own personal academic record to position yourself to achieve your greatest success.

Let's move on to Step 3 where you will need to Own, Understand and Align as well as include your own personal college preferences while continuing to stay in your own personal academic lane.

Step 3

Thoughtfully Identify the College "Parameters"

Identifying Fit Colleges

Choosing the right college to attend is one of the most important decisions you'll ever make. So, making a good choice is very important because it will have major life implications. Therefore, when choosing your "Best College Match" you want to consider colleges that are in your academic lane and suit your "style" as an individual.

Fit =   Relative Comparative Record + Personal Factors

(Your Aligned "Academic Profile") +Personal Factors

"Identify" colleges where you can feel completely free to stretch your wings and grow as a student and a young adult.

The 10 Biggest Personal Factors In Choosing a Great College

The ten biggest personal factors in choosing your "Best College Match" are listed below to help you decide which personal factors are most important to you.

1. College Major

2. Educational Quality

3. Admissions

4. Financial Assistance

5. Retention & Graduation Rates

6. Type of Colleges

7. Size

8. Student Demographics

9. Location

10. Intangibles

College Major

The first thing you need to do is determine if the colleges you are interested in actually offer your specific major or intended major if you're undecided. If your interest is in something widely offered like English, History, or Psychology, you'll have a wealth of colleges to choose from. However, if your academic interests are more focused, like Astrobiology, for example, your choices of colleges will be more limited. It's amazing how often this simple notion is overlooked and students end up enrolling in colleges they have no reason to attend.

Educational Quality

The most obvious yet, too often, overlooked part of choosing the right college is the institution's educational quality. Not all colleges or college students are created equal. In the US today, there are some 4,000 or more colleges.

Therefore, even though there may not be that one "perfect" college, if you choose one that possesses a strong academic and social connectedness then you are more likely to succeed. Where you go to college absolutely makes a difference, so look for a win-win college experience.

Admissions

In deciding which personal factors are important in choosing your *"Best College Match," admission is hands down the #1 most important of them all.* Because no matter how great the fit, if you are not accepted, then the fit is of absolutely no consequence.

Admissions is an all or nothing proposition--either you're accepted or not and in the same respect either you win the scholarship or you don't.

Therefore, strategically apply to your "Best College Matches," as well as for the right scholarships, but do so with the knowledge that the outcomes do not define you as a person.

Financial Assistance

The reality for every student is that the cost of college must be paid for in some form or fashion regardless of where you attend. Additionally, the vast majority of college students will need some type of financial assistance to cover the cost of attending college.

However, there is a large variety of resources for students to obtain college funding, including federal, state, college, and college related programs available to help defray the monetary cost of college.

The responsibility is on you the student to research and apply to the organizations that could best help you secure funding for your college education.

Although there are no guarantees of financial assistance, there are many options available to students from a myriad of backgrounds, where **those who are most successful at obtaining college funding are the most proactive in making their financial needs a true priority as part of their larger college search.**

Our advice is to start early, research-research-research, and network with all sorts of individuals who are of the same mindset, those looking to receive, give, and connect students to money for college.

When it comes time to secure college funding, it is not the time to be shy!

We have included a list of resources that will help in your college search so visit http://www.bestcollegematch.com.

Retention & Graduation Rates

Too often, unduly emphasis is put on going to college (unfortunately, often any college) and not nearly enough emphasis is put on graduating college in a timely manner (from the right college) with minimal debt.

Therefore, having a good understanding of a college's retention and graduation record should be an important part of choosing your "*Best College Match.*" Even though there are no guarantees, being aware of this information does offer some indication as to how effective that college is when considering these factors.

Types of College

Do you need a small, liberal arts college where you get to know your teachers, or would you do better at a large university with a faster pace? Answer these questions "honestly" for yourself, and you'll know for sure what type of college would fit you best. Each student must find the type that "FITS" for him/her. Look around and have fun with it.

Size

The size of the school also factors in when searching for the "*Best College Match.*" Would you rather attend a small university that creates a close-knit connection with teachers and peers? What about a bigger school that offers a wider range of extracurricular activities? Or would you prefer something in between. It's all up to you. What do you like? Which size of school would best fit your learning style?

Student Demographics

Which type of basic student demographic profile would be best suited for you? This is a personal decision that again requires an answer from the "New You." Again, this is a personal fit question that you will have to answer for yourself.

Location

As much as any other factor, the geographical location of your college could definitely help in determining your overall satisfaction of your college career as well as the quality of your daily experiences.

When deciding which colleges you might like to attend, ask yourself where you'd like for that school to be located based on your personal preferences.

Would you want a big city, a suburb or a rural environment? Would you prefer seasonal temperatures or a more moderate climate? Would you prefer to be in the Northeast, Midwest,

South, or West? Do you prefer living by a large body of water, in the mountains, or on the plains? Would you like to stay close to home or move away? You're going to be there for four years, so it's important.

Intangibles

The big ten biggest personal factors in choosing a great college is offered as a guide to help steer the process of choosing colleges that will be great for you as you complete your college search. However, many other personal considerations can be factored into choosing your *"Best College Match."*

Some additional factors might include but are not limited to:

☐   Prestige or College Rank

☐   Study Abroad Opportunities

☐   Strong Internships

☐   Research Opportunities

☐   Greek Life / Party Scene

☐   Sports Programs

Depending on what your interests might be, these additional factors will require consideration when deciding which college to spend the next four years of your life.

The Four Types of College Fits

Based on your Relative Comparative Record and your own Personal Factors you are looking for a college that is your *"Best College Match."* Of which, there are 4 types.

Best College Match Fits

Relative Competitive Record

	High	Higher
Personal Factors — Great	Specialty Fit	Highest Fit
Personal Factors — Good	Moderate Fit	Selective Fit

Specialty Fit (High Relative Competitive Record – Great Personal Factors) – colleges that offer a fit based on a student's particular "specialty" or exceptional talent, like athletics, or artistic ability or debate prowess.

Highest Fit (Higher Relative Competitive Record – Great Personal Factors) – colleges that offer a fit based on a student's exceptional academic merit, and or a complimentarily strong personal and academic resume.

Moderate Fit (High Relative Competitive Record – Good Personal Factors) – colleges that offer a fit based on a student's solid academic and extracurricular record as compared to their general student applicant pool.

Selective Fit (Higher Relative Competitive Record – Good Personal Factors) – colleges that offer a fit based on a student's very strong academic and personal record as compared to the general applicant pool with colleges that are in very high-demand.

Admissions & Scholarships 101: "The Admissions Game"

Admission and Scholarship committees utilize a narrowing down process when selecting potential applicants.

At first, they consider the applicant's "Academic Profile," which consists of qualifying those who meet the basic requirements based upon those students' academic competencies and performance. After you pass the "*initial qualifier*," as we like to call it, your application moves on to the next step for further review.

As a reminder, the four most prevalent criteria (initial qualifiers) used to assess an applicant's basic qualifications are:

1.   Grades in college preparatory classes

2.   Grades in all classes

3.   Overall rigor of the curriculum

4.   College board exam scores (ACT/ SAT)

Although most of the application decisions are made initially based on your *"Academic Profile,"* decision committees must frequently look deeper into the application, particularly when an application is of interest or borderline in order to learn more about the applicant.

How Do Colleges & Scholarships Use Your Applications

How do they come to this decision to make this type of judgment about you?

This is done through the other very important part of your overall application package that contains more subjective information about you, like your interest, talents, and achievements, which should all be very well documented through the inclusion of your essays, letters of recommendations, class rank, extracurricular activities, special talents and skills, volunteerism, work history, travel history, interviews, awards & recognitions.

College and scholarship committees use this type of information both objectively and subjectively, in deciding whether the applicant is the type of student who displays the personal character they desire.

The "tricky part" for the colleges and the applicants is that the colleges are primarily making their decisions based upon objective information. Their decisions are to a lesser degree "tempered" by a much wider varying degree of additional non-standard information like the aforementioned class rank, written essays, interest in their college or award, letters of recommendation, extracurricular activities, special in-demand skills and talents and interviews.

Extra Information Really Matters

Upon successfully passing the initial the academic qualifier of grades and scores, your additional information will be reviewed to put your application into real consideration for a chance at success.

No one knows when or if his/her application will ever make it into true contention for admission or scholarship award, but if you are going to submit an application, always submit the absolute best application you possibly can.

If you're going to commit limited time, then you must do quality work when completing the application process.

Your job as the applicant is to convey as high an academic competency and personal character as is possible using every helpful piece of information available to effectively enhance your overall application package.

The committee has to make a decision and it is your job to explain to them why they should decide that you are the best person for their school and or scholarship. Therefore, you must supply the documents that show exactly who you are and how choosing you would be great for the both of you, a true win-win.

If you've done your college selection homework using the *"Best College Match"* process, your story should be straight-forward, consistent, and compelling.

"Don't waste your time applying to colleges or scholarships that do not represent the right 'Best College Match' for you."

As you are well aware, competition for admissions and scholarships for colleges are fierce. Therefore, to best position yourself for success, it is imperative that you understand what the requirement standards are, as compared to your personal credentials, when applying to colleges.

Remember!

The "Best College Match" basic rule of thumb for submitting applications is that your *"Academic Profile"* should be aligned with the college's *"Application Profile"* so that your *"Relative Comparative Record"* is equal to or greater than the average among all student applicants before you consider of any additional non-standard support documentation.

Additionally, remember that it is your application and you always have the ability to increase or decrease the alignment of your *"Academic Profile,"* to increase or decrease the probable strength of your application.

Character Always Counts

When it's heard, there's no substitute for a great story. So, if you want to find your *"Best College Match"* you have to do two things:

1. Make sure you apply to the right types of colleges & scholarships based on your personal "Academic Profile."

2. Make sure your record is supported by a strong story of additional documentation for those making the approval decisions.

Think of it this way, when it comes to applying for colleges and or scholarships, assume that every application is going to be strong – or else they wouldn't have wasted their time to apply– so, the objective becomes how to make your application stand out among a sea of great applicants?

Strive to connect your story and let your story be consistent with your goals and ideals for college. Make sure that it's being communicated effectively in your application. It's the story you convey. Tell a great story. It matters.

So, tell a tale of yourself that displays, demonstrates, connects and shows extraordinary consistency around who you are appropriately throughout your essay. Your essay can include in school and out of school achievements, volunteerism, interviews, work experience, letters of recommendation as well as high demand skills that can be linked together and make you unique. You must tell a story that will matter to that college and or scholarship committee for which you are applying. **Your answers must address the specific questions which are asked on the application**.

These things could be the deciding factor in winning admissions and funding packages.

Identifying Fit Colleges

In this section, you'll begin the process of identifying your "Best College Match." This process can be fun, but fair warning, you need to put as much time and energy into this particular part of the entire "Best College Match" process because your end results will, to a great extent, depend on how well you are able to identify colleges that are in your academic lane AND also ones that offer you the personal factors you would want in a college.

Remember, your personal *"Academic Profile"* should be at least greater than, or equal to 50% of each college or scholarship average applicant. When identifying your possible "Best College Match," you should follow the below steps:

1.   Complete the My Personal College Factors worksheet located on page 45. This will help you

outline the basic personal factors you'll be looking for in identifying your *"Best College Match."*

2. Research lots of colleges to start. It's a good idea to identify some 10 – 20 *"Best College Match"* possibilities because as you begin to compare them, you will eliminate many of the choices for various reasons. Have some fun and search widely, even looking at colleges that you wouldn't think you'd normally consider. Developing a strong idea of what is available and what you like and dislike is invaluable in finding your *"Best College Match."*

3. For completeness as part of your search, you should consider a couple of strong for certain schools where your "Relative Comparative Record" is upwards of 80% or 90% of the average. In addition, you might consider those schools that might be as low as 25% to 50% as your <u>dream colleges</u>. Add both types of colleges to your *"Best College Match"* list, just in case because there are no guarantees either way.

4. Once you're satisfied that you've identified your strongest *"Best College Match"* by accurately aligning your *'Academic Profile'* AND your college personal factors, enter your identified *"Best College*

Match" on the – My Personally Compatible Colleges form on page 46.

5.   The "*Best College Match*" fits and or scholarships should reflect the colleges and scholarships you actually applied to at a base minimum. It has been our experience that as you are doing your research other college and scholarship opportunities will present themselves and as such when and where they make sense you should absolutely apply for them as well.

My Personal College Factors

Major / Interest: (Offered)	Yes	No	
If Yes, List Major			
Educational Quality	Low	Medium	High
Admissions Selectivity	Low	Medium	High
Financial Assistance:	Low	Medium	High
Retention & Graduation Rates	Low	Medium	High
Type of Institution:	Public	Private	
Size:	Small	Medium	Large
Diversity & Demographics	Low	Medium	High
Location	Urban	Suburban	Rural
Close to Home	Yes	No	

Intangibles

Prestige / Ranking	High	Medium	Low
Study Abroad	High	Medium	Low
Internships	High	Medium	Low
Research Opportunities	High	Medium	Low
Greek Life / Party Scene	High	Medium	Low
Sports Inter / Intra	High	Medium	Low
Other Personally Special	High	Medium	Low
List: Other	High	Medium	Low

My Personally Compatible Colleges

1 _____
2 _____
3 _____
4 _____
5 _____
6 _____
7 _____
8 _____
9 _____
10 _____
11 _____
12 _____
13 _____
14 _____
15 _____
16 _____
17 _____
18 _____
19 _____
20 _____

Now it's time to make your *"Best College Match"* a reality by preparing your winning admissions and scholarship applications.

Submitting Your Winning "Best College Match" Applications

Simultaneously while identifying which colleges and scholarships are your *"Best College Match,"* you'll also need to be completing the below *"Best College Match"* forms to have your *"Best College Match"* information ready in advance of every application you'll be submitting.

All the information can be found in the *"Best College Match"* addendums on page 81. Please stop and take a minute to look through them. It's crucially important!!!

1. BCM Application Requirement and Deadlines

2. *'Best College Match'* College Choice Ranker

3. Best College Match Price Template

4. BCM Admissions & Scholarship Basic Documentation

5. BCM Home Team Documentation

6. BCM Parental/Guardian Information

7. BCM Letters of Recommendation Information

8. BCM Extracurricular, Community Service, & Volunteer Activities

9. BCM Awards, Honors, & Recognitions

10. BCM Student Resume Template

11. BCM School Profile Document

12. BCM Financial Aid Documentation

13. BCM Essay Manager

14. BCM Personal Photo File

15. BCM Envelope System

16. BCM I Got It, I Got It, I Got It Documentation File

Gather as much of this information in advance because, regardless of the colleges and or scholarships that you'll be applying to/for, 1) most applications will require much of it, and 2) having it ready, in advance will help your entire application process be easier and more efficient.

Fill out all the addendums as completely, accurately, and thoughtfully as you possibly can. It's worth the upfront time to prepare this very useful, quality, and much needed information. So, when you do need it, is all in one place where it can be quickly accessed, tweaked, and used, again and again.

Our son used these forms and won over a million dollars in scholarships and a paid corporate internship.

So, we have every confidence that you will find them useful too.

These forms will help you stay on top of your application requests, while, at the same time, convey your absolute best personal "win-win story" for every college and scholarship application.

We believe that if you follow the "*Best College Match*" 5 step process and accurately develop your "Personal Profile," and pick strong personal "*Best College Match*" fit colleges to apply to, you will have a higher probability of success in having your additional non-standard information more closely reviewed. Thus, you will increase your chances of gaining sufficient funding and attending the school of your choice.

Furthermore, we highly encourage you to invest ample time and energy into the completion of the *"Best College Match"* Addendum documents because they could make or break your chances for acceptance into a particular college or winning scholarships.

Let the selection committees know exactly why they are your absolute *"Best College Match"* by submitting consistently strong essays, letters of recommendation, awards, interest, talents, and in-demand skills that solidify you as a great candidate for their college or scholarship.

Tell a great overall story about your character beyond the numbers alone. Describe through your documentation your strongest attributes and characteristics that make you special and different as a student and a person.

These things, provided you have used your *'Academic Profile"* effectively to "stay in your own academic lane," can truly be part of the deciding factors in winning admissions and or scholarships.

Don't Miss This!

Far too many strong applications are unsuccessful in gaining admissions or winning funding because they are submitted to colleges and scholarships that are not their "*Best College Match*."

There is a lot of information on how to prepare an application for admissions and scholarships that focus on the "how to apply" versus offering the benefit of the "why to apply" which is the strength the "*Best College Match*" process.

Therefore, please leverage all the information you can in putting together your strongest "*Best College Match*" college and scholarship applications.

Know "why" you are applying to those specific colleges and scholarships because over and above the "academic profile," the admissions and awards committees want to know that too.

Get those applications completed on time; there are deadlines, you know.

Now it's time to see how your "*Best College Match*" applications, acceptances, and awards will financially suit you in our next step.

Step 4

Carefully "Procure" College Funding

Procuring Your College Price

Finding your "Best College Match" price is one of the most critically important components of realizing your "*Best College Match*." Therefore, when procuring your "*Best College Match*" price, apply to the colleges and scholarships where you have a strong "Relative Competitive Record" and a higher probability of admissions and acceptance where:

Price = "Relative Comparative Record" + "$ Rewarded/Awarded"

(Aligned "Academic Profile"   +   "Sources & Amounts of $")

The good news is that you've already done this by identifying your "*Best College Match*" fit colleges where you aligned your personal "*Academic Profile*" for higher acceptances at colleges and scholarships that met your personal preferences.

The even better news around procuring your "*Best College Match*" price is that, unlike college admissions . . .

Paying for college is _not_ an all or nothing proposition.

The reality is that you, like most college students, will need to obtain some form of outside funding to pay for your "Best College Match" from multiple sources. Although every student's financial situation is different, varying parts of the ten basic sources of college funding can be used to fund your *"Best College Match"* price.

The 10 Sources of College Funding

At *"Best College Match,"* we want to help every student obtain his/her *"Best College Match"* price from the college funding sources that are most widely available, that have realistic requirements, and that are the least expensive. Because...

___All sources of college funding are not created equal.___

It "pays" literally to investigate your "Best College Match" price because the sources and amounts of potential funding varies greatly.

Therefore, when procuring your *"Best College Match"* funding, it is always important to apply to those sources that are most widely available with realistic requirements, and the lowest cost to you based on your overall "Relative Competitive Record," or *"Best College Match"* fit.

The ten sources for college funding are listed in order from highest to lowest benefits because not all sources of college funds are available to every student. In addition, not every student is going to meet the eligibility requirements for every source of funding, nor is every source going to be economically feasible for every student.

1. **Non-Institutional Specific Scholarships** – are largely available from many different sources, come in varying amounts, and are awarded for numerous standards of excellence across a wide variety of disciplines, most of which can be used at any given college.

2. **Institutional Merit Based Scholarships** – colleges want to attract and obtain the best students and are willing to offer top students scholarships to attend their schools. These institutional scholarships can range from very small amounts to the proverbial "full-ride" scholarships, which pay for the complete cost of attendance as well as room, board, books, and fees. Although these scholarships are non-transferable, if that school is a good fit, attaining a full-ride scholarship would be desirable.

3. **Institutional Student Aid** – many colleges, in addition to scholarships, offer financial assistance packages to potential students for a variety of reasons, depending on the strength of the college and its recruitment focus. Work-study on campus jobs would be an example of Institutional Student Aid.

4. **Extracurricular / Athletic Scholarships** – special talents and skills such as music, arts, debate, or athletics offer limited scholarship opportunities for those students with these "extra-ordinary" types of talent on a partial to full basis.

5. **Federal Student Aid** – such as Pell Grants and the Federal Supplemental Educational Opportunity Grant awards assistance based on eligible family income guidelines and are not available to all students.

6. **State Student Aid** – varies by state, and generally offers both merit and need-based awards based on individual state guidelines and award amounts.

7. **Paid Internships** – are a fantastic way to gain practical career-related work experience while earning income to supplement your college

education. They are available to all students but are awarded on a competitive basis.

8. **Family Assistance** – direct monetary assistance from the family is a great source of college funding. However, not all families are financially positioned to assist their college students monetarily, so this aspect is dependent on the individual family's ability to pitch in.

9. **Part-Time Employment** – acquiring a part-time job to earn money to help support college-costs is another avenue for many, if not all, students.

10. **Student Loans** – the reality is that these days the cost of college is so expensive that many – sometimes too many – students take out loans to pay for college when they shouldn't. Student loans should not be your first or only avenue to pay for college. Students should seek other forms of assistance first, and utilize loans to supplement the difference when needed. Students should also develop a payment plan to repay the loan as quickly as possible.

Based on all that we've previously discussed and the 10 sources of funding combined, will offer four types of overall funding.

The Four Types of College Funding Prices

Best College Match Price

	Relative Competitive Record	
	Lower	*Higher*
Great	In Demand Price	Merit Price
Good	Standard Price	High Demand Price

Funding Awarded

In-Demand Price (Lower Competitive Record – Great Relative Award) – typically, students who fall into this area represent some type of "specialty" or exceptional talent where it could be for super star athletes, great artists, debaters.

Merit Price (Higher Competitive Record – Great Relative Award) – typically, students who fall into this area represent those at a given college who are the best of the best scholastically with the strongest "*Academic Profiles*" (i.e. the highest quality applicants). These students are offered large scholarships and other strong award funding packages from the college because of their exceptional qualities.

<u>Standard Price (Lower Competitive Record – Good Relative Award)</u>– typically, students who fall in this area represent the majority of students at a college who have average "*Academic Profiles*" and resumes.

<u>High-Demand Price (Higher Competitive Record – Good Relative Award)</u> – typically, students who fall in this area represent students who have an otherwise strong "*Academic Profile*" but are not being funded accordingly. This situation usually happens most often when great students apply to premier or prestigious colleges where the demand far exceeds the supply; therefore, even if a student is accepted into a premier college, because the demand is so high, the funding awards can be equally in high demand, where many students who are accepted may not always get the best funding awards.

College Funding Packages - Scholarships & Financial Aid Packages

To get a visual of the *"Best College Match"* price awards packages for Tammy & Tommy see the illustrations for both students on pages 61 and 63.

'Best College Match' Price Tammy Example

Student Name: Tammy

College / Scholarship: 'Best College Match' Price

College Cost

Tuition:	$ 9,750.00
Room & Board:	$ 7,710.00
Books & Supplies:	$ 1,000.00
Fees:	$ 196.00
Other:	$ -
Total College Cost:	$ 18,656.00

College Funding Sources

Non-Institutional Scholarships:	$ 1,000.00
Institutional Merit Scholarships:	$ 17,460.00
Institutional Student Aid:	$ -
Extra / Athletic Scholarships:	$ -
Federal Student Aid:	$ -
State Student Aid:	$ 1,000.00
Paid Internships:	$ -
Family / Personal Assistance:	$ -
Part Time Employment:	$ -
Student Loans:	$ -
Total College Funding:	$ 19,460.00

Net College Price

(Total Cost - Total Funding)   - $ 804.00

Tammy has done well with understanding, aligning and selling her record and earned (2) scholarships totalling $17,460 from her 'Best College Match' and an additional $1,000 scholarship from her participation in outside clubs. Also, Tammy has earned another $1,000 in state incentives. Thus, she will have her entire cost of college funded and put $804 a year in her pocket for expenses.

Not too bad for the privilege of attending a strong state university.

'Best College Match' Price Tommy Example

Student Name: _____Tommy_____

College / Scholarshi____'Best College Match' Price_____

College Cost

Tuition:	: $ 48,900.00
Room & Board:	: $ 6,330.00
Books & Supplies:	: $ 2,500.00
Fees:	: $ 750.00
Other:	: $ -
Total College Cost:	: $ 58,480.00

College Funding Sources

Non-Institutional Scholarships:	: $ 10,000.00
Institutional Merit Scholarships:	: $ 35,000.00
Institutional Student Aid:	: $ -
Extra / Athletic Scholarships:	: $ -
Federal Student Aid:	: $ -
State Student Aid:	: $ -
Paid Internships:	: $ -
Family / Personal Assistance:	: $ 4,000.00
Part Time Employment:	: $ -
Student Loans:	: $ -
Total College Funding:	: $ 49,000.00

Net College Price	
(Total Cost - Total Funding)	: $ 9,480.00

Tommy has done well as a scholar and has been accepted into one of the best colleges in the country by earning (2) scholarships totalling $35,000 from his 'Best College Match' and $10,000 in additional outside scholarships.

Additionally, Tommy will receive another $4,000 from family contributions annually. However, if he is to attend this great institution Tommy will still need another $9,480 per year for 4 years or $37,920 in total student loans for the highly regarded college credentials upon graduating from this top college.

So, Tommy will ultimately have to make the life choice that is right for him.

Thus, when it comes to funding your *"Best College Match"* price...

"Paid for" can be very different than what is actually "Paid For."

The key is to look to the "New You" to know which "Paid For" is right for you.

Your Personal College Funding Packages

It's more efficient when structuring your "*Best College Match*" price funding package to use the enclosed "*Best College Match*" Price Template in the Addendum to:

Add Personal Information

1.   Start with the amount your family will provide for college after having a family discussion around support for college.

2.   Get your FAFSA, as required by all colleges, out of the way as early as possible because the required dates are subject to change. An update will be required once you've filed that year's taxes, so revise your FAFSA at the same time you file your taxes and be done with it. Your eligibility and or award will be determined for you.

3.   Add to your total how much you might personally contribute to your college expenses, through current and or future part-time employment.

4.   In advance, familiarize yourself with all the state aid that is available for you so you can apply before the deadlines.

Where the "Best Match Price" is Made!

1. Research and apply to the Non-Institutional Scholarships that you think you have the highest chance of success, based on your "Best College Match" fit and given your "Relative Competitive Record."

2. Apply for early admissions and Institutional Scholarships to the colleges that you think you have the most competitive chance of success based on your "*Best College Match*."

3. Apply for early admissions and Institutional Aid with the colleges that you think gives you a competitive edge based on your "*Best College Match*" fit.

4. Apply for early admissions and Extracurricular Institutional and Sports Scholarships to the colleges that you think fit your "*Best College Match*" based on your ability, talent, and skills.

5. Research and apply to schools and other entities that offer paid internships in the field of your interest that you feel you could have a competitive chance to be successful.

When & Where It Makes Sense

1. Consider potential student loans ONLY after all other college funding sources have been 100% exhausted. The loan should only be a part of the larger college-funding package. Student loans should never be a first option and should be completely avoided if at all possible, but at the same time in certain situations, student loans can be a valuable part of your *"Best College Match"* price.

Note: Your personal *"Best College Match"* price will be financially rewarded much like gaining college admissions acceptances that will depend on your 'Relative Competitive Record' as compared with the concurrent college or scholarship *'Application Profile'* applicant pool you are competing against.

Therefore, when it comes to procuring your *"Best College Match"* price, if you have chosen to apply to your *"Best College Match"* fit colleges and scholarships as outlined in Step 3, your overall "Relative Competitive Record" will be as great or greater than most when you apply. In this sense, you should gain larger *"Best College Match"* price packages to pay for more of your schooling.

Thus, the value of understanding, properly aligning, and selling your *"Academic Profile"* to actualize your *"Best College Match"* price will be a benefit, and is nearly as important as having a great academic record alone.

Step 5

Honestly "Pick" the *'Best College Match'*

Now for the fun part, hang in there you're almost done!

It's been quite a journey and the hardest parts have already been done where you've:

1. Mastered your personal self-awareness

2. Accepted ownership of your academic proficiency

3. Thoughtfully identified your college parameters

4. Carefully procured college funding

5. Now it's time, to honestly pick your own personal *'Best College Match'*

Haste Makes Waste

We know it's been a long process and you're pretty much ready to get this whole college thing over with, but we just want to encourage you to stay with the process just a little bit longer.

You've worked so hard, we'd hate to see you give up, or freak out now and lose everything you've labored so hard to get.

"Let's pick one and go home."
Semi, Coming to America

Please be careful at this point in the process because everyone is tuckered out and ready to pick one and be done. Therefore, now is actually the time to be extra cautious in evaluating which of your funding types offer the *"Best College Match"* for you.

Your *"Best College Match"* is obtained when you balance your *"Best College Match"* fit and your *"Best College Match"* price funding packages where:

Best College Match **= FIT + PRICE**

Therefore, the combination of your 'Best College Match' fits and your 'Best College Match' prices – i.e, your college acceptances and the concurrent college funding awards – would now represent your 'Best College Match' college choices.

Having stayed true to the process, you should now have a list of colleges that meet the criteria you established as most important. In addition, this list should include those colleges that offer the best funding options so that you can enter college without burdensome financial concerns which will lead you to greater academic success.

Through the *"Best College Match"* 5 step process, the type of college you ultimately pick as your "Best College Match" will fall into one of 4 *"Best College Match"* college types where:

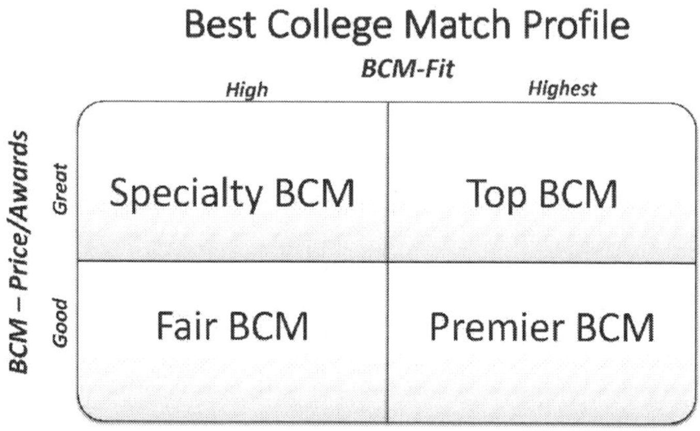

Best College Match Profile

	BCM-Fit	
	High	Highest
Great	Specialty BCM	Top BCM
Good	Fair BCM	Premier BCM

(Vertical axis label: BCM – Price/Awards)

1. **"Specialty" Best College Matches** (High Fit & Great Awards) – offers great financial prices for students with exceptional talent

2. **"Top" Best College Matches** (Highest Fit & Great Awards) – offer great financial prices for exceptionally strong academic merit

3. **"Fair" Best College Matches** (High Fit & Good Awards) – offer good financial prices for average relative academic merit

4.   **"Premier" Best College Matches** (Highest Fit & Good Awards)– offer good financial prices for exceptionally strong very high relative academic merit

You'll Be Fine, Honestly Pick.

Please know and have confidence that . . .

When picking your "Best College Match," your personal understanding and what's ultimately best for you should *drive* your decision.

Therefore, if you need to take the road less traveled, it will certainly make all the difference in your "Life's Success."

Use the *"Best College Match"* Ranker in the addendum on page 84 to complete this exercise in determining your *"Best College Match"* College.

1.   Complete the ranker with all the information requested including the BCM Profile Type information.

2.   Based on what you now know and have achieved, and after completing the "Best College Match" process, rank your possible choices on your ranker in descending order.

3.   As the "New You," personally review your choices for "Best College Match," and if necessary, seek further consultation to help you with your decision.

4.   Pick the *"Best College Match"* offer that is the best overall fit and price for "YOU"!!!

<u>Congratulations</u>, you've picked your own personal "Best College Match."

The Final Word

There is, ultimately, no right or wrong decision because every student has his/her own personal life compass. What appears to some as a better fit, might be passed over for what appears to be a lesser choice, depending on what that student sees as best for him/her individually.

For example, there are some "Tommys" who, having been through the "Best College Match" process ended up as a "Premier" college match. They were perfectly content with paying a premium at a particular college because they personally felt the additional cost was worth the investment.

On the other hand, there are "other Tommys," who will choose another "Best College Match" because they personally cannot justify the additional cost.

It's all up to you.

Congratulations again, and best wishes on choosing your "Best College Match."

Conclusion

Staying True to the Spirit

There will be tough days applying for colleges and scholarships, and tougher days in life when you are feeling completely overwhelmed, but you have a personal obligation to persist, and to not only work harder but to work smarter also.

Persistence makes you who you are. We think former President Calvin Coolidge said it best when he said:

"Nothing in this world can take the place of persistence. Talent will not: nothing is more common than unsuccessful men with talent. Genius will not: unrewarded genius is almost a proverb. Education will not: the world is full of educated derelicts. Persistence and determination alone are omnipotent." - Calvin Coolidge

If you are to reach your optimal "Life's Success," you must possess the character to persist by having the confidence to put your competence into action especially when life gets tough.

Therefore, in all you do for yourself, in college and in life, persist and stay true to the spirit of your greater Life's Success. Choosing the right college is only a part of Life's

Success, but the process of doing so is as much of an art as it is a science.

In life, the more you understand about yourself and your needs, the better prepared you are to make proper decisions for your life."

The truth is different for each person because it depends on a person's interpretation of where he/she situates him/herself at that current moment in life. Based upon your understanding of your competencies and confidence in your abilities, knowing yourself is paramount to making decisions that work "Best" for you.

Life offers no guarantees for anyone, even those students who have realized their *"Best College Match."*

Therefore, the absolute best that any of us can do is to remain true to who we are as people by staying true to the spirit of what we know to be "Best" for us.

Put what you know to be "Best" for you into action while always persisting to understand more.

If you don't have understanding or understanding enough, then go get it! The power of understanding is out there for you if you are willing to work hard for it.

Thus, as William Ernest Henley so appropriately states:

"You are the master of your fate: you are the captain of your soul."

It is your personal duty every day to remind yourself of these very powerful words as you travel the great journey of life.

Remember! You determine where and how far you will go in life because of the investment you've made in yourself through keeping the spirit.

Life's Success is all up to you – you can do it.

We hope this book helped.

Now go forth, boldly and prosper into a new unknown world and achieve all the Life's Success your heart can handle.

Addendum

BCM Application Requirements and Deadlines

Admission / Scholarship: _____

Application Deadline: _____

Application Requirements	Requested	Completed
Application	_____	_____
Tour Completed	_____	_____
High School Transcripts	_____	_____
ACT / SAT Scores	_____	_____
Letters of Recommendation(s)	_____	_____
Extracurricular Information	_____	_____
Awards & Honors	_____	_____
Resume	_____	_____
School Profile	_____	_____
Financial Aid Information	_____	_____
Essay(s)	_____	_____
Personal Photo	_____	_____
Pre-Paid Envelopes	_____	_____
Other	_____	_____
Submitted On:	_____	
Application Status:	_____	
Approved / Declined:	_____	

Best College Match College Choice Ranker

BCM - Colleges Acceptance / Scholarship	Net College Cost	BCM Profile Type	Choice Rank
_____	_____	_____	____
_____	_____	_____	____
_____	_____	_____	____
_____	_____	_____	____
_____	_____	_____	____
_____	_____	_____	____
_____	_____	_____	____
_____	_____	_____	____
_____	_____	_____	____
_____	_____	_____	____
_____	_____	_____	____

'Best College Match' Price Template

Student Name: _____

College / Scholarship: _____

College Cost

Tuition:	$ _____
Room & Board:	$ _____
Books & Supplies:	$ _____
Fees:	$ _____
Other:	$ _____
Total College Cost:	$ _____

College Funding Sources

Non-Institutional Scholarships:	$ _____
Institutional Merit Scholarships:	$ _____
Institutional Student Aid:	$ _____
Extra / Athletic Scholarships:	$ _____
Federal Student Aid:	$ _____
State Student Aid:	$ _____
Paid Internships:	$ _____
Family / Personal Assistance:	$ _____
Part Time Employment:	$ _____
Student Loans:	$ _____
Total College Funding:	$ _____

Net College Price:
(Total Cost - Total Funding) $ _____

BCM Admissions & Scholarship Basic Information Documentation

*High School Transcript (supplied by student)

*ACT/SAT scores (supplied by student)

BCM - Home Team

Building a long-term, strong home, school, and community network of individuals to help support and guide your journey to find and fund your BCM is "Invaluable." Most adults, given a student's honest pursuit of furthering oneself, are almost always willing to provide support.

Therefore, build a strong team over time with folks who really know you and can offer the highest level of tangible support that will help you the most when it's really needed. Adults, especially educational professionals, know those students who are sincere about their academic careers and have formed strong relationships with those students because of their dedication to their education.

Thus, there can be no wonder that these students of the many who will need guidance, documentation, and letters of recommendation will generally tend to get better, stronger, and faster support than those who do not have this greater relationship, or who have not taken their school career as seriously as they should have before it was time to apply to college.

Teachers and school professionals are humans too, and they are keenly aware of their students' overall ability and sincerity through the college application/scholarship process.

So, start early, be forthright, and build the types of relationships with the people you will need come college application time. The bottom line is that, in most cases, these adults have a lot of sway in either being a tremendous asset or yet another hurdle in your quest to obtain your BCM. If they are solidly on your team, they can offer very helpful suggestions, ideas, and resources to support you.

BCM- Home Team Documentation

Student Name: _____

Parent / Guardian: _____

School Support

Teacher	email	_____	phone	_____
Counselor	email	_____	phone	_____
Principal	email	_____	phone	_____
Coach	email	_____	phone	_____

Non School Support

Program Director	email	_____	phone	_____
Non Profit	email	_____	phone	_____
Extra Curricular	email	_____	phone	_____
Church	email	_____	phone	_____
Mentor	email	_____	phone	_____
College Rep	email	_____	phone	_____
Alumni / Group	email	_____	phone	_____

Peer To Peer Support / "The Buddy System"

BCM student participants	email	_____	phone	_____
Classmates	email	_____	phone	_____

BCM - Parental / Guardian Information

Name: _____

Relationship: _____

Mailing Address: _____

Home Phone: _____

Cell Phone: _____

Email Address: _____

Name: _____

Relationship: _____

Mailing Address: _____

Home Phone: _____

Cell Phone: _____

Email Address: _____

College Legacy Information

Name: _____

Relationship: _____

Year Graduated: _____

BCM – Letters of Recommendation Information

Recommendation For (Name): _____

Recommender: _____

Requested On: _____

Supporting documentation supplied to recommender on: _____

1. Resume
2. Pre-Made & Paid Envelope   _____
3. Requested Deadline Date of   _____
4. Specifics About the Request   _____

Actual Deadline Date: _____
Completed & Submitted On: _____

Recommendation For (Name): _____

Recommender: _____

Requested On: _____

Supporting documentation supplied to recommender on: _____

1. Resume
2. Pre-Made & Paid Envelope   _____
3. Requested Deadline Date of   _____
4. Specifics About the Request   _____

Actual Deadline Date: _____
Completed & Submitted On: _____

BCM - Extracurricular, Community Service, Employment & Volunteer Activities

Strategy: List all of your extracurricular, community service, employment and volunteer activities. Rank them from highest to lowest order of importance and record them in the table below.

Date(s)	Activities, Community Service and Employment / Position	Hrs / Wk
Example: Sep '14 – Present	Winning High School Debate Team, Team Captain	17

Gregory and Opal Dawson

BCM - Awards, Honors & Recognitions

Strategy: List all of your awards, honors, and recognitions. Rank them from highest to lowest order of importance and record them below.

Scope*	Awards / Honors	Grade	Date

Scope* e.g. International, National, Regional, State, Local School

BCM – Student Resume Template

Use the information from the BCM Extracurricular and Awards Template to complete your resume.

Name:

Future Educational Goals:

Current Educational Status:

Awards & Recognitions:

Extracurricular Activities:

Work Experience / Volunteer Service:

Personal Interests:

BCM - School Profile Document

Many colleges and scholarships will require that a copy of your high school's "School Profile" be submitted as an application requirement from either you or from the school directly.

Request a copy from your counselor and keep it on hand for when it may be needed.

(Add School Profile here)

BCM - Financial Aid Documentation

All colleges and some scholarships will require financial information directly related to the amount of "Financial Aid" available to their student applicants and will ask for the following forms as verification.

1 FAFSA: Free Application for Federal Student Aid

2 SAR: Student Aid Report

3 CSS: CSS / Financial Aid PROFILE
      (sometimes requested by certain colleges)

A good story is worth its weight in gold – or should I say college admissions and scholarship awards – committees read or at least start reading thousands of essays every year; the vast majority of which they never finish.

Make certain your essays are some of the few they actually do read completely. Your story, if it's actually read, can mean everything; it's one of the few ways a committee can best get to know who you are.

Don't try to impress the reader; simply share things you've learned about yourself. The committee wants to understand how you think and how you might benefit their college and or scholarship investment.

There are a thousand pieces of advice available for and on how to write the best college essays. Research and use that which you think is most appropriate for you.

Write and rewrite a lot of essays! Have them reviewed by many different people, especially those on your BCM Home Team, and by all means, make sure you answer the question that was asked!

BCM – Essay Manager

Essay For (Name): _____

Prompt: _____

Word Limit: _____

Started On: _____

Due By: _____

Reviewed Last On Date(s): _____

Completed On: _____

Essay For (Name): _____

Prompt: _____

Word Limit: _____

Started On: _____

Due By: _____

Reviewed Last On Date(s): _____

BCM Personal Photo File

Many colleges and or scholarships will ask its applicants for a personal photo in the form of either a small printed picture or a .jpg file as part of their application requirements.

It's a great idea to keep them both on hand just in case.

(Add your personal photos here)

BCM Envelope System

	Recommender	College / Scholarship	Date Due
1	_____	_____	_____
2	_____	_____	_____
3	_____	_____	_____
4	_____	_____	_____
5	_____	_____	_____
6	_____	_____	_____
7	_____	_____	_____
8	_____	_____	_____
9	_____	_____	_____
10	_____	_____	_____

A considerable amount of information that you will be required to collect, have completed and or forwarded from other third parties like principals, counselors, teachers, coaches and others whom you've asked for additional information will often be required to return information on your behalf directly to the college and or scholarship committee.

As these people will in all likelihood be completing the same types of information for a lot of students, its always best to make it as easy as possible for them to remember you in the best light possible.

So make it easy on them and provide them with a fully completed envelope with their return information and the address to where that documentation is to be sent along with the proper attached postage and supply your recommenders some much needed help in the process.

Best College Match

BCM - I Got It, I Got It, I Got It Documentation File

(general file for extra just in case documentation, notes etc.)

List of Items in my BCM general information "catch-all" file

1 _____

2 _____

3 _____

4 _____

5 _____

6 _____

7 _____

8 _____

9 _____

10 _____

Made in the USA
Columbia, SC
10 June 2018